The Toast

Mark Young

LBP
Luna Bisonte Prods
2021

The Toast by Mark Young

Cover image
slata u 4
by Alberto Vitacchio

Book design: Mark Young & C. Mehrl Bennett

ISBN: 9781938521751

Luna Bisonte Prods
137 Leland Ave.
Columbus OH 43214 USA

www.lulu.com/spotlight/lunabisonteprods

CONTENTS

cont'd

cont'd

Some of these poems have previously appeared in:

A New Ulster, Adelaide Literary Magazine, Adjacent Pineapple, Anti-Heroin Chic, Big Bridge, BlazeVOX, Brave New Word, Communicators League, Die Leere Mitte, eccolinguistics, Empty Mirror, E·ratio, experiential-experimental-literature, First Literary Review – East, former **P**eople, *Futures Trading, Hamilton Stone Review, Have Your Chill, Indefinite Space, Ink Pantry, Local Nomad, Marsh Hawk Review, Moss Trill, New Mystics, NOON: Journal of the short poem, One Sentence Poems, otata, Otoliths, Oz Burp 7, Past Simple, Rasputin: a poetry thread, Read On, Sewer Lid, Stride, SurVision, Synchronized Chaos, The Curly Mind, Unlikely Stories, Utsanga.it, Word For/Word, X-Peri, Yellow Mama, & Ygdrasil.*

My thanks to all the editors.

A Recipe

Start with a word. Any word.
Or a phrase, even if it's in
Greek or Latin & so obscure
that you have to go back & look up
the meaning of it after only a couple
of days. Start with anything; but
if it seems to be leading to a
dead end, then fence it off with
*   *   *   *   *   *   *
& move on. With another word
or phrase. A sentence even. It
doesn't need to relate to what's
gone on before, doesn't even
need to make sense. Some
thing may fall out of it, several
things perhaps. Or reprise the
first phrase, invert it as if it were
a Bach canon. Even if you still
can't remember what it means
you might recall what you meant
by it. It gives you pause either
way, a breathing space in your
line of thought; & from here on in
you can improvise, embellish, go
off on a tangent, imagine you are
Jean Genet writing the script for a
travelogue. Add anecdotes. Quote
or misquote from others. Leave
road signs for later travelers
but cover them with graffiti until
the original meaning is obscured.

Let stand for thirty years.

One for the Border Force

So maybe you take the chance
& walk out across the sand &
into the sea. Maybe
they won't notice you there
among the dervish gulls, think
you're a rock or a resting
seal. & even if they do they
probably won't care. Their
job is to stop people
from coming ashore, not to
stop the malcontents from
leaving. Just don't turn around
& try coming back.

A dog in space

is the foremost Kabuki actor of the modern age
was anxious to baptize me in the Missouri River
does not cling to San Diego "like sheets to the skin in summer"
offers a unique chance to see the highlights of Australian sheep-shearing
has speeds similar to ADSL technology, which is 25 Mbps or slower
sang for two years in the chorus of the New Orleans Opera Company
really didn't have anything to do with my refrigerator
operates 100 preschools that are located within public schools
has discovered an affinity with horses
gets lag spikes & stuttering after an hour playing gta v on pc i
compiled 80 photo book ideas that will help inspire your next project
has nobly stood on a rock outcropping since 1925
was hurt after falling from a trapeze during a Cirque du Soleil performance
has been digitized by Google from the library of Oxford University
helps car accident victims fight for full compensation
has taken full control over all the Aleppo districts abandoned by rebels
teaches dance to children in a fun, safe, & encouraging environment
looks set to radically change attitudes towards mobile homes
did not die of a mysterious head wound while on a stroll with its owner
did not attend the annual White House Correspondents' Association dinner
does the majority of its business on the Internet
has ended up in the Swan River during peak hour traffic
needs to be able to interact with the audience & involve them in the
experience

retrograde condensate

As a flockmeister / most
of her caprices involved
the works of Patrick White.

Hands neatly tucked away out of sight.

It is very important at the
beginning to send out a DVD
of a Nuclear Blast — deliberate
capitalization — *to demonstrate*
the true character of retro-
grade dogmas. (Amos, 5:24)

MICE — meetings, incentives, conventions &
exhibitions — become a hazard for drivers.

Try adding more information.
Unfortunately, too many com-
puters are unsure what that is.

Is said the strength of Biscuit,
of Crunt & Biscuit, lies in his
opening his mouth real wide.

The similarly green grasshopper

When asked about 'life on the road'
Pound said he felt that the container
it came in should be concave like a medi-
eval mirror, thus bringing the seen image
into center focus. In further social
commentary, he also noted that turning
insider status in upon itself could be
considered as a utilitarian good, but

should be visually inspected even when,
through its regulatory framework,
access was denied. Now the largest
karaoke community in the country is
in tongue-range of the frog gently
edging upwards on the outside wall.

the usual pit-head working

I shot this great buck in Kansas.
How does this object know
what to do apart from an in-
stinctive desire for authenticity?

: map / symbol / gold :

A parent in the winter says that the
feminist movement didn't actually
help women. Cost accounting is
considered to be a part of parenting.

: beginning a hierarchy? :

The Marketing Manager at Turf per-
formed acoustically. A need for nothing
can be a reason to relax consistency.
Or does that only apply to synthetics?

: visit our site to buy.

The following is a list of characters
in the DC/Vertigo title *Hellblazer*.

to assist their graduating

Walk towards City Hall &
around the corner to find an
entrance to the Go Gator ride.
You won't be disappointed! In-
side is a crust/neocrust band
with cello & dual male/female
vocals, & fireplace solutions of
exquisite implants that recently

hauled the Vatican over the coals.
Shop at Burlington & all you will
find are pawned shields, now
over-painted with red pigments
on a black background to hide the
designs that were there before.

the tragic mode is archaic

Undermined by public mistrust,
the ethics of language testing
has become a tragic spiral now
facing a small sausage that can
significantly harm sperm quality.
Such an awesome template! It
throws caution to the wind &
into the Penola river whether or

not a tweet was sent. Can impose
the least possible uniformity on
observed conflict & parking at-
tempts with a choral performance.
The subject was later found shot
to death on Renegade Mountain.

Post-Credits

We're chomping at the bit.
Have glimpsed some
kind of killer alligators &

hurricanes in nostalgia-
baiting cameos. You DO
have a current robot file

to work out if it actually
is a cypher? Without it, "no
information is available

for this page" will display,
& speculation over the next
season can only carry on.

Transportation

The terms of
his natural
life included

an embargo
on the use
of artificial

intelligence.

Bushidō

Lollipop-men curdle the sky. Else-
where anchovies, but smaller than

the prototype. In a moment of
impetuosity, the Sage claimed

the desert was his friend. Went
out into it, was never seen again.

Just before Tucson

A kingfisher on the wires, a
dead pig by the side of the road.

"Such a bellicose armada," says
my mother as she pauses between

apoplexy & Appalachia, to smoke
another contretemps, & wait for

the next epiphany to roll around.

Daisy irae

A small shiny-black beetle
crawls across the inside
of the car window. The field
is being prepared for rice. We
watch a riverboat move in waltz
time along the highway. A stop-
light sings silently to itself.

Rotation

Choosing to walk this way
though other paths are easier.
In with the old, even if the
futures market seems to pre-
dict that genetically modified
crops are the way to grow.

But where will the money come
from? For the poor especially
it does not grow on trees that
do not grow. Landscapes of
drought or flood, playing fields

where insurgents surge to preach
religious intolerance. Nothing
gets through. A single variant
good – if that's the term – for a
single season since new seeds need
to be bought to plant another crop.

a nearly impossible malware

Benign activities take place
in secret. The governess
sends others to be exe-
cuted in her place. It is
purely aesthetic. Scientific
methods cannot measure

the effect that has on his
pysche any more than it
can quantify the emissions
of the caribou grazing in the
lower paddock. He wakes
up sweating. Fever abounds.

Those / with skin / in the game

The wearables industry is full
of older adults who did not
go to high school. Interviews
are everywhere, posted anony-
mously, usually by errant
children. Their kaleidoscopes
have missing or blurred pages.
Plus poor pictures, often in mono-
chrome instead of the surround
sound they were designed for.

been on the road for quite a while now

He was feeling virtuous
at having gotten up early
& eaten some over-
priced fruit & yogurt. Now
he is scrolling quickly through
social media, trying to stalk
his ex. He finds no trace of
him, only photos of martyrs
& zealots along with hazy
shots of sea & ponds & an
eye-opening, previously un-
told, history of civil rights.
That annoys him; so he
tries trolling footballers &
French chefs & leaving racist
abuse on their various sites. An
idiot pop-up informs him
nobody goes home empty-
handed. He couldn't agree more.

breathless carols

The neighborhood sparkles
with elaborate home & yard
displays. It surprises me at
times that absinthe retains
its demonized reputation.
Still, my homemade chicken
has become so iconic it turns
a random walk, even over

strident metal percussion, in-
to a filter used to dynamically
populate fields with a default
value. Shaving is no longer an
easy task, now that you have to
bring your own chair & candle.

Making cryogenic ice cream

Whimsical objects. Pumpkin
logo. A study on trumpets.

Serious again. Orbital satellites,
migration of metals. The field is

sparsely drilled. Framed prints.
Gradient color. Low stress

abrasion. Wakes to a dystopia.
What does water vapor mean?

brand positioning

A spectrum is a
collection of scalar
values with its
black curve being
an analog of
the momentum.

Which is why a
fixed dimensional
living space may
wish to concede
that abacus marble
or rock counters

can take the place
of trees when
considering the cause
for some cases
of partially-
working proteins.

parking was metered

A particular place, a
limited amount of time,
a forest with minimal
cultural lighting. No re-
flection in any of them.
Composite screens can
be a distraction in these
situations unless you
keep a plug-in handy.
Adaption will be imp-
ortant at times like this.

census

Now, after Time's helix,
are these two / one &

the same? *A spectre is*
haunting Europe — Karl

Marx. *A specter is haunt-*
ing Texas — Fritz Leiber.

termite entropy

Tunnel patterns can be
broken down into groups of
physically unrelated types
of barcode tags. San Diego is
a candy store for smugglers.
Here is a look at some of our
in store stock for this Easter
weekend. There's a special on
trained CIA-backed marksmen
wearing Huggies Pull-Ups to a
Disney Junior Dance Party. Out-
let shopping is ALWAYS a good
idea. We are open regular hours.

implementation / seems to / me too visionary

With the fusion of barbaric
heuristics & association rules

uprooting may mean moving
to another mainland where

talks between six world powers
& Iran have agreed verbs were

most frequently directed toward
the location of the syntactic.

paradigm a dozen

The grunge music scene is
teaching old neurons new
tricks. I now have blueberries
on my cereal while two dozen
girls learn about innovation
first hand, getting to witness
a cyborgian dancer. It's a
scene of midmorning disarray
& excitement that has the citi-
zens of Gettysburg panicked—
Lincoln is coming on the right
day. I'm scared stiff, but why
should I be alone. I bring in my
investors & show a 40-minute
video of an avalanche bearing
down on a ski vacation in the
Alps. It exacerbates their fears.

raiment

I am wearing a soft cashmere sweater —
ocelots try to hide behind my eyes.

I am wearing a Model T Ford magneto —
Vesuvius erupts & buries Pompeii.

I am wearing gloves & the touchscreen is unresponsive —
I'm not quite Imelda Marcos, but the comparison has been made.

I am wearing the minute hand of an Audemars Piguet watch —
demagogues accuse me of being soft on slavery.

I am wearing old clothes this Chinese New Year —
from where I sit, "antipodean culture" seems like an oxymoron.

I am wearing an account manager with a colorful fashion sense —
my cellphone rings, & illustrates the concept of mortality.

I am wearing a spearmint velvet blazer as a marker for intelligence —
later I will walk down to the lagoon to look for the pelicans.

single-serve liturgies

A railway line runs im-
mediately behind the
parietal lobe. The placebo
effect could make pictures
of classical architecture
affective as stimulus mate-
rial. Split-brain syndrome
using different lags provides

empirical motivation for
some true effects to exist
at particular intervals. Our
RV got rear ended by a hit
& run driver. Unlicensed
work is non-free by default.

Fill / loosely & / do not compact

With experience, this copper-alloy piece can be used to create a product that includes all the processes involved in harvesting, production, transportation, & construction. It eliminates all extremes of elaboration, but forces you to leave behind your familiar house, street, & neighbors; & prompts a defection from fixed meaning through the use of non-sequiturs — start off with Magritte & move on to the navigational abilities of the prostate, from Derrida on to the venture capital industry.

trajectory as far as

What we retain of the
movement is its structured
form. Any steady increase
in template performance
can be processed by the
use of microcontrollers
or some contextualized
analysis of migration &

language diversity. Else-
where, work permits are
only offered to those with
a separate income flow or
the ability to access behind-
the-counter medicines. The
intransigence of light she
found difficult to cope with.

she calmed down after she'd finished talking

Anger had got the better of that
"o" often found at the ending
of Australian nicknames. Else-
where, over the fence, two young
girls sing each example of that We
will, we will rock you line from
the Queen song. They are dread-
fully out of tune, as if part of

a conspiracy whose aim is to
utilize misshapen counterpoint
as a way of moving minds away
from — not so much the current
pandemic but the paucity of the
responses to it. Negative energies
accumulate in the corners. Even
feng shui can't drive them away.

It's important to be hetero if you're school captain

I am riding the funicular, one that runs
on waste water. The elephant on the seat
in front is busy getting a facelift, & fighting
off the advances of a diplomatic courier
who still has a pouch attached to his nose
piercing. Diatribes are being offered at
bargain basement prices with a 10 cent
surcharge refundable when you return the

container they came in. I turn my back on
them, preferring the corner desk slightly
outside the apothecary's monocular visual
field. A mime climbs on to the trapeze. I
cannot make out what they are saying to
me. I gesticulate back at them. They smile.

Déjeuner sur Les Demoiselles

When I can, I put goat cheese on
my philanthropy. It opens all
sorts of doors, from bondage parlors
through to bishopscourts. Picasso
joins in with me, murmuring that
not all bullrings are created equal
though it's hard to tell until you
prise your eyes apart. I don't know

what he means but won't admit
it. He tends to get annoyed at what
gets lost in poor translations. A wood-
pecker turns sawdust into snacks
like trail mix, nuts, & crackers. I spit
in its eye, then offer it a lollipop.

User pays

Relevance, or the
scattering of benefits
to any- or everyone

so that they pay
attention. A band
comes marching down

the street. No-one is
there to greet it since
no benefit accrues.

Mist

"I have the same con-
cerns." She put her phone
back in her bag. It was

nearly one o'clock. He
cleaned the ashes out
of the barbecue pit. The

sky was darkening with
rain clouds. It was time
to put the ice cream out.

A line from Woody Guthrie

Real men now care about
skincare. They perm their
hair, have their eyebrows
shaped. It's been going on

for over a year, part of a
major breakthrough in the
global effort to ban conflict
diamonds. Some say it's an

effect caused by the sun, or
by the Fed dropping rates
in an attempt to kickstart
its rocket program which

is rapidly running out of puff.
Parallels are drawn with the up-
surge in classic texts now being
Kindled. Old notions die hard.

transient gryphons

The reduction of nitrate led to a
low-level dynamic revolution in

some game scenes. Turns out knee
& shoe buckles cannot overcome

nature; nor can boilers & coffee
pots. But even though laden with

timber & wood goods from British
ports in America, any well placed

vessel can shoot down a drone by
using a prototype laser weapon.

jars full of bathtub gin

We made haste & scrambled
eggs. It was icy for us; but, hand-

wrapped in brown paper &
tied with a silk ribbon, became

great everyday home décor.
You know how the song goes.

a less frantic piano

We were unable to save
the boy. The variability
is caused by differences
between individuals,

cannot be represented
exactly as a decimal. The
easiest measure is its
range — take ten if you

did not check any of the
squares. May not be
copied, scanned, or dupli-
cated, in whole or in part.

Polymerase

I am traveling through
time dressed up as an
ocarina. Someone is play-
ing me — their breath
smells like snowshoes.

axing proves

You do not have to settle for
the town mahjong hero — here,
let me take the keyboard. Lady-
bug y Cat Noir have a past &
revisionist views of events, but
even the most skeptical analyst
does not believe all the goodwill
has been completely wiped out.

So, there is nothing to forgive. The
protagonist enters a new world
where early voting polling places
are not yet available. She is still
quite mobile but gets tired easily.
Is three weeks of it too long?

Cryogenesis

It was a short-lived
thing. She trusted
her instincts. The man

seemed to take stock
of the situation very
quickly. He looked

at her, said: *I don't*
have a plan. She smiled.
I have enough for two.

Remembrance Day

It is eleven minutes past
eleven, on the eleventh day
of the eleventh month, &

I am driving over the Bur-
dekin Bridge remembering
Proust & wondering if it's

not too late to start a band
which I might call *Mark et*
Marcel et Le Temps Perdu.

The Night of the Caribou

There are fewer than ten days
left. We are heading out for a
post-dinner stroll before contin-
uing on to breakfast. The status
quo has rusticated & cows now
graze along its edges. In exchange
for food we have been given
shovels to clear away the expanse

of bovine shit that has accumu-
lated since the last patsies they
could find departed. Our native
land recedes in memory as the
inability to return there increases.
So far we have seen no caribou.

Some *geographies*

Sardinia

The short-sleeved
polyester shirt
is now too tight
for the mountain
goat, & serves only
to create a mis-
leading impression
of what one can
expect from an Age
of Enlightenment.

Nogales

He carried a-
round with
him an entire

repertoire of
the movements
of wild-raised

ergomomically
sustainable
deckchairs.

Basra

Redeployed personnel
from the redundant
media so cherish
what they have

they are ready
to fight the state-
owned railroads
from house to house.

Lake Hamlagrøvatnet

Intelligent robots are fictional
pieces of equipment
primarily used to treat
sleep apnea. But if you're

going to travel through
time, then tractor parts
are something that a snorer
cannot live without.

Shaanxi

The traditional view
is that the earliest
advocates of change
in traditional China
received crucial
support from the
bad science that
produced song titles

like "the poet
continues his fight
for life" & "my first
taste of government-
run health-care on
a massive scale."

Hortense, GA

She sighed as she
poured the last of
her cardamom seeds
into the mortar, moist-
ening them with a little
alcohol—last year her
mother said the alchemy
was a bit too dry. The
proselytization of reality tv
means its constant
advertisements take scant
time to start to suffocate.

Gdansk

Skeptics say there is
no easy way to test

claims that any loosely
defined subset of furry

ponchos, fur-lined flip-
flops, & sweater sets

adorned with broaches
will continue to float

when cream is added
to the pumpkin broth.

Arnhem Land

Modern Living & The
Ancient Way of Life

is a boutique fund
manager focused on

delivering long white
sandy beaches & azure

waters to researchers
tracking feral cats.

Cachapoal

Chile's warm valleys
compete for customers
by offering comfortable

dumpsters with balconies

& yoghurt containers
printed in the color
of your favorite rose.

Winnipeg

Grain orientation
in electrodeposited
nickel is a type of
comb added by bees
to prevent most
mediated plastic
deformations.

Blantyre

Why not explore the
moonrise in an adult male
category 'C/D' resettlement
prison modeled after your
mother's ancestral home?

Bogantungan

A low level plat-
form & a spartan
waiting shed
funded by the

Commonwealth
due to the war
effort. He looked
at his watch &

noted the time.
Span class="cap-
tion-caption." The
bridge collapsed.

Concord Town

So maybe there
does come a time
when everybody freezes
their painted face
in place & goes
scurrying big-
footed off to the
showground to
find the circus
of their desires.

Alexanderplatz

Such attitudes appear
very rarely; but the
American position at
the Berlin Conference
made it very clear that vision of
a car driven by a 76-year-
old woman who mistook
the gas pedal for the
brakes & plunged into
the chilly waters of Lake
Washington looked kinda
tropical & Caribbean.

Rhode Island

A woodcutter & a
priest have just
played to a half-full
tent with their songs
about the crybabyblue
color of fibrillation.

Nederweert-Eind

If you're looking for
a pre-1963 registration
plate, as in Tingting
May's passionate novel
*The employment opportunity
is with a State Farm Agent,*
then *going to be the earth's
surface would be the fact
under water,* is most
propably a misprint.

Puerto Padre

Don't think that growing
a pair & being combative

is destructive, that this
foolish ban can stop me

from coming back. The
organizing principle is

competition, not the philo-
sophy of mathematics. She

paused & pretended to think
about the price of tech stock.

Bibra Lake

Later, in the middle
of both a storm &
the afternoon, Barb's
Butchery opened with
a vow to protect the
urban lakes & water-
ways from domestic
violence by coal tar
sealants & level paths.

Galicia

A Marine holds an
umbrella on the famous
medieval religious pilgrimage
to Santiago de Compostela.

Very nuts-&-bolts.

He might not look as pretty
as Beckham, but he can play
football. His services include
all aspects of waxing & tinting.

Plesetsk

The function of slow
clicks is less clear
than the advantage
in launching a
spacecraft from
some higher latitude.

New York City

The new pro-breast milk
policy stigmatizes colored
glass & provides less leg
room for creatives to put
their ideas out on the table.

Faubourg St. John

It is rumored that
the Welsh stoner metal
band regarded as the

pioneers of the genre
actually began their
career playing quadrilles

at the St. Jean Fort in
New Orleans some time
in the early 18th century.

Teluk Ambun

A green man on a bi-
cycle, with a huge
body & tiny bungalow,

followed the peloton
on the route along
Trikora Beach. She

was peaceful & air-
conditioned. Nobody
had much money at

the time. Logical
errors are the hardest
kind of errors to find.

Khyber Pakhtunkhwa

The notion of a souffle
gambolling through
sun deckled woods
recalls US-provided

images of drone
strikes on isolated
villages in Waziristan
that purport to

show that no
animals were harmed
in the filming of
the commercial.

Little Village

The flow increases &
becomes channelized,
causes a cheetah on the
prowl in the 26th Street
neighborhood to attack

& viciously maul a party
of retired Chicago Police
officers on their way to
the Pride Parade at
Octavio Paz School.

Cheyenne

Even though
widely regarded
as obsequious but

essentially inoffensive
the noisettes of
Wyoming beef sirloin

were eventually
beaten to death by
a young British

couple recently
returned from back-
packing in India.

Istanbul

Women's made to
measure flare pants,
with an aroma

of light oak
& dark fruit,
were built by

Numarine in Gebze
& intended to convert
the U.S. Nuclear Naval

Fleet away from endangered
pecan turtles & across
to red velvet cupcakes.

Languedoc

By exposing their
one-dimensional
approach to the re-
cycling of electronic
waste, the exhibition
of Camargue cowboy
images just opened
at the Aquarium pre-
sents proof positive
of the negative
side of traditional
male behaviors.

Fayette County

A life crisis, a major
transition. The water
had risen. Based on the
Mayer cluster expansion
of the partition function,
enough water to swim
in. Just as we did in Iraq,
we can execute this

transition responsibly.
Sandstone crenellations &
a sort of Victorian-Edwardian
outhouse will benefit from
these considerable computa-
tional savings; & we can
afford to dine with family
& friends in Lexington.

Houston

The weight of past defeats
underlies the pre-Copernican
dogma that smoking a whole
brisket in just 6 hours will
slash the current flying
time in half. One wonders
what all the fuss was about.

Palau

Scaffolding creates remote-
ness, mixes crossbows with

sand to improve moisture
retention, even after the

safety has been re-engaged.
An electrolyte imbalance

means the dome light keeps
flashing; visible seaweed in-

dicates low water level. Soak
the kelp in a jacuzzi to keep

it androgynous & the vision-
ary crabjuice business viable.

Coober Pedy

Don't be discouraged by
the peculiar C++ lambda
syntax—the second function
of any draftsman is to recognize
that Southern Iron's principal
project assets are the Peculiar
Knob Prospect, & that occasionally
you'll get the odd bug when
hacking some stuff onto Bitcoin.

Cincinnati

Seurat's use of long-
term storage for his
broken lines of color

was a formal endeavor
to ensure that a wet
weather box always

remained in the top
right hand corner of
his website even if

paddle boats didn't
make a comeback or

hypothesis testing was
temporarily unavailable.

Sacramento

The news reports are some-
what unclear; but either

ten chipmakers or ten
chipmunks are uniquely

positioned to benefit from
the explosive growth in

Big Data analytics caused
by the fact that most of the

former Japanese picture
brides were working at

the time they initiated
divorce proceedings.

Roscommon

In isolation, adipose
tissue reduces the
microcosm that is Ireland

into a gated community
of various migratory &
local birds who share

a propensity to commit
mass suicide when new
epidemic diseases appear.

Mesa, AZ

There are no originals,
just tremulous foliage & an
indefinite suspension from
practicing law. Our universe
is one of many, as purely
objective journalists keep
pointing out, slyly inserted into
an angry dialog between
the fruits of war & the stereo-
typical gender portrayals of
most third-person pronouns.

Fukuoka

The heaviest of metals — when
mixed with a small percentage of
coconut fiber — is delicately de-
signed to permit the use of wet paper
in failed nuclear power plants.

Honiara

Five reef islands
believed to have
been lost completely
to sea-level rise

have just been re-
discovered alongside
a pair of air jordan
flight club sneakers

inside a St. Thomas
Aquinas reliquary re-
cently rescued from a
burning van in London.

Harlen Beach

A traditional paradigm
causes difficulty when
swallowed if the image

has bled through the sub-
strate. Assassins in black
clothes are notoriously

hard to detect. Paying
smugglers seems safer if
there's little hard data.

Tyrnavos

Phallic ritual is a
literary genre that blends
aspects of natural rubber
& cognitive therapy, &
turns them into car-
niverous autos, some
comic, some tragic.

Bandung

Uber, with its rich
colonial architecture &

world class secular
education, has, along-

side the baby boom,
played an important

role in the history of
postwar population.

Ciudad Bolivar

Now that the instruments
of the national orchestra
have been turned into
mulch for the cacoa
plantations, it's easy to
see why US president
Donald Trump's decision
to send a task force of
egregious windmills into
Venezuala to resolve the
country's political crisis
was anathema to the
local musical community.

Antalya

One of the hubs in this so-
called cradle of civilization is a

treasure house of circum-
cized single USB ports. It also

includes a kitchen that uses an
obscure cosmic emanation known

as "fast radio bursts" to facilitate the
production of their artisanal craft

beers which are now available
in cans & bottles or on tap.

Qaraghandy

CCTV allows the large
Coyote Canyon framed print
currently occupying wall
space in a small Melbourne
based design studio
to also be on display in a
place considered by many
in the former USSR as
the middle of nowhere without
having to be anywhere near there.

Hafencity

The Hamburg Farmer's
Market is now in a
cocoon of scaffolding
with much shorter
blast times & a lower
overall cost per hour.
Boiler slag is an in-
expensive media.

Serengeti

Any history of man-
animal interaction
catches the spotlight
as an imagined
threat. We speak of it
only in images &
parables, focusing on
known conditions
of life rather than the
mental architecture.

Decatur

By the time we left the
village, it was raining
legibly. The adhesive

that she was wearing,
one that joins laminate
to any other floor sur-

face, turned out to be
a poor substitute for a
constitutional scholar.

(end of *geographies*)

A line from Hannah Weiner

I brought my dog on a cool
day. 1060 people were here
in the sweeping lobby of
the hotel. It took my breath

away. Most of these slaves
were once held in New York:
a new trafficking reality is
challenging; the geographical

scope of activity has been
expanded to explore new
markets. Incoherent realities
out of a nation that thinks

itself civilized. Weiner's
phrase no longer a Legerian
depiction of the geometry of
an excursion to the beach. Now

become a symbol for sex worker
solidarity. Begun with a march
at the Venice Biennale. Carried
on under the red umbrella.

Streaming

She was in the foyer. It
was late at night before
she managed to reach her
personal security team. They
would be with her within

the hour. She dropped her
purse on the divan. Coffee
was what she wanted, but
with no power, how could
she make it? Seagulls were

everywhere though the sea
was far away. Her neighbor
was practising for a coming
concert. She played cello.
There were no witnesses.

the character killed off early

I have a charcoal grill made
of hand painted high-quality
resin with several different
mounting options. It's really
important to let others know

what one possesses — I've
been hiding who I am for so
long. Feedback is necessary,
especially now that I'm part-
icipating in so many Zoom

meetings courtesy of my new
gooseneck camera. Motors
must be single phase, familiar
with the key knowledge dot
points, & printed on thick 100

pound quality paper. Weak
AI, neither measured nor bil-
led, could cause disruptions
in the electric grid. Please
enter your model number.

I knew nothing of screenplays

The strident laughing of her cellphone caused the azaleas in the front yard to be trampled underfoot. That followed hard on the heels of a recent cover of Motorhead's *Stone Dead Forever* that also went nowhere. Next morning was full of reverberations & repercussions. Such a pity she had never dated drummers.

I find it difficult

The Emperor was standing

near my bed. He is plain &

simple, but beautifully made.

A bowl of almonds

The road ahead is full
of a glare her eyes had
never become accustomed
to. Animal corpses on
the tarmac. An ubiqitous
photographer who, for
the moment, is still
standing or standing still.

She looked up, looked down;
realized where the ancients
got the names of their con-
stellations from. Music of the
90s wafting across her nos-
trils caught her unawares.

Et in Arcadia, ego

The Wagner was in full voice
when she arrived. She made
the words out & mouthed
along with them for a few
moments. *Er naht: sie bringen
ihn getragen.* So, *Parsifal.* She

couldn't be bothered hanging
around. Grail stories had be-
come too common, too far-
fetched, too often pitched at
future cinematic treatments.
Star Wars &/or *Star Trek* now

more her go. Classical themes:
& the music isn't bad, either.

Ecumenical

She woke up to a room
full of ikons. Coptic saints
scowled down at her, the
occasional orthodox Greek.
Was fairly certain they

hadn't been there when she
went to sleep which meant
somebody had ignored the
do not disturb sign she'd left
on the doorknob. A cablecar

ground to a halt in the corner,
equidistant from the gilded
images of Habib Girgis &
John Chrysostom. Another
intrusion. Then a knock on

the door, followed by the
uninvited entrance of a
wimpled nun. "The reliquary
is open," she intoned. "What
would you like for breakfast?"

A line from Henry Ford

Focus attention on the
illegal gun. Know how to
ride a bike. War is a risky
get-rich-quick scheme

if you're afraid of the stock
market. The French terror
maniacs met often with
poetry, had an infinite

capacity for some modern
Mexican poets, particularly
a wild-eyed Latina whose
exposé of the links between

Kentucky coal mines & organ-
ized crime explains why rich
people have such chicken-
shit long term memory.

Gas guzzling

The rising price of
petroleum products

has persuaded me to
convert my elderly

laptop from running
on hi-octane to diesel—

this way I get more
letters per liter. But

the increase in emiss-
ions has caught the

attention of the pol-
lution control board

who have started to
scrutinize my every

word. That's the down-
side. The positive is I have

now finally found myself
a permanent readership.

a vicarious journey

Would take out
postcards &
show me where

he'd been. Would
take out road-
maps to show

me where he's
going. I went
along for the ride.

A step away

Something small, but
always there. A street-
light amongst trees, the
joy of coming on it after
a time away. The beacon.
It is what we look for. Not
the dark foreboding & the
rattling echoes of an empty

house or the cacophony of
a light-strewn series of
familiar rooms. Too much
to take in in a single bite. In-
stead go for the bouquet,
from outside, a step away.

Meanwhile, in the path lab

The high price of silver
or a voluptuous Tamil
heroine exposing her thighs
in a provocative way are

reliable & often-used tools
to evaluate the levels of
pathogen transmission. Note
that for each given Beat Set

there is an associated Rhythm
Space. Such non-dominant self-
categorizations may reduce the
possibility of conflicting cognitions.

inappropriate calories

It's a magic number. No, not
three, which seems to have
assumed the position because
of children's shows & De la

Soul & Blind Melon, amongst
the many who have risen to
fame on the back of that claim.
We're actually unsure of what

the magic number really is. Let's
call it X, let's say it varies. Like
how many people on a bridge
before it starts to wobble. Or

how long it takes for high heels
to start hurting. Or bad style in
source code. Which means this
piece will probably not compute.

el jardin de los senderos que se bifurcan

Begin. At the
beginning don't
stop unless you
arrive at a place
you believe is
exactly where
you started or
at least shares
a common
meridian. Other-
wise keep on
going. Circularity
is a tortuous process
& not all beginnings
are the same no
matter how alike
they look. Not all
are beginnings. Some
may be. The end.

Songs to come for the salamander

Axolotls can breed whilst still remaining tadpoles.

[Hellbenders, mudpuppies, waterdogs, sirens.]

There are nine
families of salamander,
some 300 species.

Andrias japonicus
is five feet long.

[Lungless salamanders. Mole salamanders.]

Salamandra salamandra
is black with bright yellow,
orange, or red markings.

Newts.

Neoteny is the retention of some juvenile characteristics
in an animal that seems otherwise mature.

Axolotls will only metamorphose into
adult salamanders when their ponds dry up.

The salamander is impervious to fire.

A line from René Magritte

It's a bleak view of hu-
manity. Facing eco-
logical collapse, Freddo,
plus a whole host of

Cadbury characters, went
beyond science to shine
a spotlight on transgender
issues, using their jittery

art-punk guitar buzz to
offer a frayed life-line to
the most vulnerable people.
The snowoman wonders

what the world offers them
outside of that. An ability
to handle subzero temper-
atures? They have that already.

Animal Farm

It's the cantaloupe
for sure—all the
other animals have
been locked up for
the season, served
decaffeinated tea & do-
nut holes, listening to
piped Berlioz—but we've
rung the paleontologist
just in case. Evenings
are like that. Forms
dismembered &
rearranged in a
different order, a
new light cast, things
picked up after several
decades absence, their
corpses pored, pawed
over. I'd never really
thought about it
before, but it's the
obvious in Eliot that
gets me angry, "coming
over the Starnbergsee"
indeed, as if there
were some other
direction to arrive
from, light rain or not.

Croft / Craft

Pertinence. Soft words
hold little of it. Better
to pick up stones to
make your point &
leave the phraseology
to bricklayers. That's
what they do after all,
the regular lines, off-

set against each other,
in natural cadence, a
start / a finish to it all,
looking for that last un-
settled, previously unen-
cumbered, piece of land.

delta cockroaches

Plumbing lines should really
be treated with or treated to
video clips of Michael Jackson
from the days of the Jackson
5. Except. The browser does

not currently recognize any of
the video formats on offer since
YouTube has **completely re-
moved** its Flash player code
from its site. I load up my boat

with pretzels & set sail for the
Azores in the hope that hedge-
rows of blue hydrangeas will
recognize a kindred stranger.
I Want You Back propels me

along even though it's on its
last legs; but, at sea, it doesn't
matter all that much. A mael-
strom beckons to me, but my
pretzels kick in & minimize it

in the bottom left hand corner
of the screen where it can whirl
impotently. Finally I reach the
outskirts of the harbor. A limo
is waiting. It moonwalks me in.

The / purpose lies / in the concept

: if required & :
is for the purpose
: of :

: dotted with :

: not for achieving :
from the relative
: comfort of his home :

: phenomena are often observed :

¡ extensive knowledge is important !

landscape with proscenium arch

Center stage is an orange caricature, a man muttering about "vicious dogs" & "ominous weapons." Something of a bully who, unfortunately, has a bully pulpit to play with, that incorporates a prompt or two from which he reads — badly & with an obvious lack of understanding of their meaning — the words of those others who he thinks, for the time being at least, are on his side. His head is cocked, like a bird listening for worms, only without any signs of innate intelligence.

There is noise offstage. Suddenly secret service agents come rushing in to the room, form a phalanx around him, & escort him to the confines of the in-house bunker. For some time there is silence, then the bird returns, tweeting incessantly.

Not all features are supported

My Snapchat isn't working.
Corn husks & potato skins
have caused it to jam by
creating a starchy paste similar
to type 1 diabetes. I need help.
Motion sensors undermine the

metabolism of my underwear.
I ring up NASA who send me
a counter-intuitive brief titled
Generating Smooth Motions For
Robotic Manipulators & Other
Palindromes. Now my teeth

start hurting. Snapchat still
isn't working. I log out of my
account & log back in as *The*
Book of Mormon tells me to
do. It resyncs my local snaps,
but with someone else's server.

vows shared, glasses raised

There is client virtualization plus
sets of customer data; yet a singular
failure to add heat — whether fire
or some other external source — is
becoming increasingly common. Racism
opens its doors. An ambient
intro of cellos greets your ears &
introduces the masses to the person
known as 'the tree man.' Calories do
count. This includes understanding.

We are faced with a massive marketing
effort in a very com- pressed time frame.
Surviving the siege would have been
sketchy at best. Many similar alloys
have been created on first tasting the
hands of humans. It's really just the
nature of largesse, terracotta, or bio-
batteries. Inscription is essential. The
one question still getting raised a lot is;
can kinaru *take the place of* misugaru?

postilion entropy

Rubato is a mathematical concept
with different cost functions,
a community-based family support initiative.
This is not a complete list of side effects.
It is a trap.
A wall gropes open.
The protagonist is corrupted.
Sylvester was very clouded over
with a vanilla bean head.

Downloaded May 6, 1872

That first morning, in the utility
room, a handful of custard apples

& a vanilla yoghurt with apricot
jam stirred through. Which should

I offer up as proof of life? The clergy
have left & I am left with the laity.

Will they let me finish my glass of water?
Nothing else has changed except the smoke

on the horizon & the corpses of pink
Cadillacs decaying in the winter sky.

an iconic trapezoid

Her legs are congruent, have
an experimental approach
to materials & colors, has
something to do with her love
of horse riding &/or those
crumbling monuments to
Pizza Hut's stylized roof &
other relics of the West's in-

dustrial heyday. Her quiet-
ness has a bell inside that
mimics the phantom noises
in the ears associated with
tinnitus. When magpies be-
gan to call she turned & ran.

I Can't Wait To Reconnect With Lilo Again

Some of you might remember me.
I was a trope once used in popular
culture, The Dark Lord rising to
gather his armies in the context
of a global mobility shift. Footage
was shot for the newscasts when
my dual citizenship situation first
arose. Add to that body- & dashcam

captures released by the police, plus
a university's private surveillance
videos. "The well is a mirror," said
a woman at the center of the fray.
"The marital relationship is not the
primary emotional bond. Rather it's
a beachfront property with uninter-
rupted views." "It's our culture," says

another, "a disturbed emancipation
with an average of 250 résumés sub-
mitted for every condo. Those false
children are cases in point." Views-
keyboard_arrow_down. The chances
of trees trapped in a prism of refracted
light surviving are almost zero. You
are so lucky being back in Belek again.

Yorkminster

A salamander gambolled in the
garden outside of where he dined
on radicchio & the deep-fried
antennae of communication satel-
lites. Elsewhere was birdsong; &
crystalized bible readings; & the
caps of elderly travelers escaping
the confines of their Winnebagos
for lunch on the run. His brow
became encased in the local
library & froze in place. None
of the proffered titles did he
recognize — not that that mat-
tered. Some languages were
never intended to become the
preferred, the common tongue.

Sacramento Daily Union, 6 January 1887

VEUfiTABLES —Potatoes—Early Rose, 90c; Nevada Snow Flake, tl 65; Nevada General I Grant, $140; River Red, B0@8Bc; Onions, I $1 65@1 J6j Cabbage, 75c(i'51; Carrots, sjc; 11mups,75c sack; bunch vegetables, \Z%c « fioi; Parsnips, 81 2D;Beets, tl;Eor<ie Radish, tiia.7cV *; Garlic. l@sc; Artichokes, 40c SR dozen; Okra, sc. BBEA_L>STITFFS—FIonr. ti 70 « bbl; Oatmeal. (3 75 9 100 s>s: Cemmeal. white and yellow, <1 8"> In 25 it, Backs, f 2 in 10 S) sacks: Cracied Wheat. 91 75: Hominy.s3so ft cwt. POULTRY—Lite 'I'uricys, hens, Wi@l4o ; gobblers, J2J<tISJjQ; Dressed, i.3c; full-grown I Chickens, «o %i" dozen: vonng Roosters, H a) V dozeD ; Broilers, J2 5033 50; tame Ducks, ttcati SO; I'ekiu. &"> 50: Teal. 7fc; Quails, $1; Hare, SI 50; Mallard', S3; Widgeon, 90c; Sprig, SI 50; Canvasback, ?::; Geese, tmi 25 p oalr; KgCT, choice CaUforrila. 25QSSO; Eastern, 19520 C i "* dosen. DAIRY PRODTJCrS-Bntter. fancy roll, 27'<;@ 30c {I a: ranch bntter, '2:>a2sc; pickled, 2u<s 21c; packed in firkins, choice, 19a>IOc; common, 12@15c: Cheese, California, 3S3>lsb: WestBra flats. 13@Uc; Martin's Cream. He. HAY, GRAIN AND FEED-Oat hay. *Bg9 V MU Alfalfa do. (>.iV) ?i ton; Bran, 810 $ ton: Middlings, 121 « ton; Barley, whole, paying 81 12; rolled, $1 80: Wheat, paying tl SO 9 cwt; W Thite Wild Oats, SI 75(3.1 85; Tamo Oats. $1 G-V Corn, paying Jl 05 » owl. MISCELLANEOUS-Seeds - Alfalfa, 9>£@loe ; liniothy, Eastern, t%%li B> i Pod Corn. © 3>i.©-la V !b; Eta Clo»er, 10@lle: Red Top, B®9c. Nuts — Chile Walnuts, new 11J 11a; California Walnuts, 13®i60; Almonds, new 143 5:; Peauute, Caliiornia, 4K@5Ha Lara (Oaliforaia). cans, 7Hrsß>£c; Eastern, S%® 93<c. Hldps, sail, light »nd medium, 8c; heavy steers, S^c; dry, 16c. Tallow, 3c. Bopfc— Sales of r'aoific coast. In New York, 25@27e; morkpt v»iu» here. 25&27 C. MEATS-Beef, s(rJs^c; Mntton, s®s>sc $ 1b; Lamo, 7c; Veal, 7<g)9c; Hogs, 2Ji©3o; lireßsed Fork, 5o; Hams, Easteru. 16c: Califbmia, 12e: Bacon, medium, 9><o; selected, lie: extra light, 12c. _

minimum energy input

The pulse amplitude of one bath-
room per bedroom suggests the
presence of premature beats; but
it's not clear what underlying
process they represent. The tests

can take months or even years;
& all you're likely to find out is
something irrelevant such as
breastfed babies are more likely
to develop jaundice because they

haven't mastered any phonological
skills yet. Skipping a heartbeat is
more serious than skipping lunch;
but the fluttering sensation that
follows has its own taste sensation.

Three French Horns

Winnebago shared a post
on Instagram, a screenshot
of some anthropologist's tale
of the deconstruction of the
phrase *a partridge in a pear*
tree by a group of pueblo
dwellers. Some individual
ideas were reported; but
essentially the consensus
rotated around two oft-repeated
questions: *where's the buffalo*?
& *why is Angela Merkel so*
often criticized on social media?

A Coptic Christian school in Frankston North has gone into administration

Police confirmed that when they arrived a man was found suffering from a lack of consumer & business confidence in global governments. A number of gunshot wounds were also discovered by MPs who were concerned a no vote at the UN would offend Middle East & Muslim communities on the fragile front lawns of their properties. This has proven that ineffective policy responses were set up in the southwest for the purpose of a large negative shock that could bring the US & global economy into recession. A law-enforcement agency called the Industrial Police has been specifically assigned to deal with unrest on fiscal cliffs & upbeat party room speech factories.

US Secretary of State Hillary Clinton named next Archbishop of Canterbury

Right-wingers don't like her because industrial production, fixed-asset investment, retail sales, electricity generation, & the beauty of the Islamic faith all strengthened more than expected last month. Police said she is a bleeding heart, with her ruminations about households in the middle quintile of taxpayers & her advocacy of renewable energy for Salvation Army shelters. Disembarking at Sydney's Kings Cross, she formed a transitional government for rebel-held areas, & will presumably serve as a conduit for inquiries on foreign aid to the opposition, & a torrent of loans to state-owned homeless men.

interaction is crucial

The most elegant inter-
pretation of quantum
mechanics states that
macrophages are re-
quired for a parallel
reality to exist; & that
can only happen if
zebrafish are the sole

peer-reviewed species
allowed to be taken out
of captivity to become
an accepted model for
neuropsychiatric studies
into tissue regeneration.

BOOM FM *

Can Face Masks Prevent You From Getting the
Coronavirus? Doctors Weight In
Lesbian Tiktoks That Made My Gayness Increase
I Show the Weirdness of My Life Through My 30 Comics
Caffeine & Breast Cancer
Kenyan MPs Shooting The Jerusalema Dance Challenge
At Parliament Building

Before You Renew Amazon Prime, Read This
A Maryland Baby Taken Off Life Support Was
Not Expected to Survive. Now She's About
to Have Her First Birthday
I Went Vegan for 10 Weeks and This Is What
Happened to My Body & Mindset
Trump's Ex-Girlfriend: I Was Flattered to Be a Trump Girl

* Bored Out Of My Fucking Mind

A line from Ada Lovelace (2)

The way he ties his ties way
too long is a science of itself,
like hoisin sauce or miso. Do
I need to spell out my grand-

father spends a lot of his
time comparing brands in the
grocery store he goes to every
Saturday? He's getting old;

so to simplify his tasks, I've
added a little bit of code
& a few dedicated function
buttons to his Zimmer frame.

Another set of anterior appendages

Anchored to the hair by
centipedes wearing
elastic sombreros, even
the most advanced anti-
rain cycling accessories

cannot avoid bringing with
them more than a hint of
biting arthropod. It dis-
plays as an inflammatory
reaction similar to that

occurring when a library's
dustiest corner is disturb-
ed. Only the addition of
mirrored aviator goggles
will work as a deterrent.

The Toast

Shortly, & with
little warning, the
pools of hypocrisy
ice over & become
malevolent. We are
back in St. Petersburg,
never having been
here before, but I
recognize the
ghosts. "Such pretty
lizards," she said, then
raised her glass in
the general direction
of the sky. *"Za vashe*
zdorovye." It was
a formal toast. No
story followed

The following books by Mark Young published by LBP are available at
https://www.lulu.com/spotlight/lunabisonteprods or spdbooks.org

turpentine, poetry, 6" x 9"
black & white interior, 100 pp., June 2020

Taxonomic Drift, poetry, 6" x 9"
black & white interior, 100 pp., June 2019

les échiquiers effrontés, visual poetry, 7.5" x 7.5"
full color interior, 32 pp., May 2018

www.ingramcontent.com/pod-product-compliance
Lightning Source LLC
Chambersburg PA
CBHW060206050426
42446CB00013B/3009